Results in Brief

Evaluation of Government Quality Assurance Oversight for DoD Acquisition Programs

November 3, 2014

Objective

Our objective was to evaluate DoD overarching quality management policies and procedures and Government-performed quality assurance oversight of defense acquisition programs. To evaluate DoD quality management practices across DoD, we evaluated top-level policies and procedures of DoD Components (that is, Military Departments, Defense agencies, the Joint Chiefs of Staff, the combatant commands, and DoD field organizations).

Findings

DoD through the Office of the Under Secretary of Defense for Acquisition, Technology and Logistics (OUSD[AT&L]) has not established an overarching quality management policy to ensure the consistent application of quality management system requirements across DoD Components.

In addition, DoD and its Components do not have effective feedback mechanisms in place to evaluate the performance of quality management system and sufficiency of policies.

Recommendations

The Office of the Under Secretary of Defense for Acquisition, Technology and Logistics should:

- Establish within OUSD(AT&L) a dedicated quality management function to provide leadership and oversight of quality management system requirements across DoD acquisition programs.

- Provide clear and concise quality management system definitions and policies for all DoD major acquisition programs that emphasize the importance of a robust quality management program throughout the entire acquisition life cycle.

- Establish quality assurance verification processes throughout the acquisition life cycle that promote effective program and supply chain quality management systems.

- Establish standardized reporting requirements for quality assurance metrics throughout DoD to obtain the information needed to detect trends, identify threats and opportunities, and evaluate program performance.

- Establish policy that ensures Defense Contract Management Agency (DCMA) policies and risk-based quality assurance oversight decisions are reviewed, understood, and agreed to by the program management offices.

Management Comments

On October 17, 2014, OUSD(AT&L) responded to our recommendations. OUSD(AT&L) partially concurred with three recommendations and did not concur with two recommendations. However, we determined that comments from AT&L do not meet the intent of our recommendations. We request that the Under Secretary of Defense for Acquisition, Technology and Logistics provide additional comments in response to this report by December 5, 2014. The following table identifies recommendations requiring additional comments by OUSD(AT&L). Please see the Findings section in the report for detail.

Recommendations Table

Management	Recommendations Requiring Comment
Office of the Under Secretary of Defense for Acquisition, Technology and Logistics	A.1, A.2, B.1, B.2, and B.3

Please provide comments by December 5, 2014.

INSPECTOR GENERAL
DEPARTMENT OF DEFENSE
4800 MARK CENTER DRIVE
ALEXANDRIA, VIRGINIA 22350-1500

November 3, 2014

MEMORANDUM FOR UNDER SECRETARY OF DEFENSE FOR ACQUISITION,
TECHNOLOGY AND LOGISTICS

SUBJECT: Evaluation of Government Quality Assurance Oversight for DoD Acquisition Programs
(Report No. DODIG-2015-028)

The DoD Office of Inspector General (OIG) conducted an evaluation of the DoD's implementation of its overarching quality management policies and procedures and on Government-performed quality assurance oversight of defense acquisition programs. We evaluated the top-level DoD Components' policies and procedures regarding quality management of the DoD acquisition programs. Furthermore, we determined if there were any gaps and weaknesses within the DoD quality management policies and procedures.

Our evaluation determined that the Office of the Under Secretary of Defense for Acquisition, Technology, and Logistics (OUSD[AT&L]) has not established an overarching quality management policy that is commensurate with the scale, cost, and complexity of the Major Defense Acquisition Programs to ensure the consistency of quality management system requirements across DoD Components. In addition, the Department of Defense and its Components do not currently have effective feedback mechanisms in place in order to affect positive change in quality management policies and processes.

We considered management comments on the draft from OUSD(AT&L) when preparing the final report. We request further comments from OUSD(AT&L) on Recommendations A.1, A.2, B.1, B.2, and B.3. Further comments should be received by December 5, 2014.

DoD Directive 7650.3 requires that recommendations be resolved promptly. If possible, send a .pdf file containing your comments to ███████████████. Copies of your comments must have the actual signature of the authorizing official for your organization. We are unable to accept the /Signed/ symbol in place of the actual signature. If you arrange to send classified comments electronically, you must send them over the SECRET Internet Protocol Router Network (SIPRNET).

We appreciate the courtesies extended to the staff. Please direct questions to CAPT. Christopher Failla at ███████████████████ Christopher.Failla@dodig.mil.

Randolph R. Stone
Deputy Inspector General
Policy and Oversight

cc:
Assistant Secretary of Defense for Acquisition
Director, Defense Contract Management Agency
Director, Missile Defense Agency
Auditor General, Department of the Army
Auditor General, Department of the Navy
Auditor General, Department of the Air Force

Contents

Introduction

Objective 1

Background 1

Evaluation Process 4

Evaluation Criteria 5

Finding A. DoD Lacks Overarching Quality Management Policy and Guidance 7

Recommendation A – Management Comments and Our Response 9

Finding B. Ineffective Feedback Mechanisms to Improve the Quality Management System 12

Recommendation B – Management Comments and Our Response 14

Appendixes

Appendix A. Scope and Methodology 17

Appendix B. Prior Coverage 18

Management Comments

Office of the Under Secretary of Defense for Acquisition,
    Technology and Logistics 19

Acronyms and Abbreviations 23

Introduction

Objective

Our objective was to evaluate DoD overarching quality management (QM) policies and procedures and Government-performed quality assurance (QA) oversight of defense acquisition programs. To evaluate DoD quality management procedures, we evaluated the top-level policies and procedures of DoD Components. See Appendix A for our scope and methodology.

Background

We initiated this evaluation due to gaps and deficiencies in overarching policy related to quality management, practices, and oversight as identified by several Government Accountability Office (GAO) and DoD Office of Inspector General (OIG) reports.

In 2008, GAO issued a report identifying quality management deficiencies in DoD acquisition programs. GAO stated that problems related to quality management system deficiencies identified in 11 DoD weapon systems resulted in billions of dollars of cost overruns, multiyear delays, and decreased capabilities for the warfighter. The following are some of the examples of programs that encountered quality deficiencies. The Expeditionary Fighting Vehicle program experienced a high number of nonconformances during assembly, which resulted in a 4-year development delay and a cost overrun of $750 million. Reliability and manufacturing deficiencies contributed to a 5-year delay and cost overrun of $117 million in the Advanced Threat Infrared Countermeasure/Common Missile Warning System. Quality, reliability, and maintainability problems resulted in a cost overrun of $400 million on the F-22A program. The USS San Antonio (LPD 17) Amphibious Transport Dock also experienced numerous quality problems, which significantly impacted the ship's mission and resulted in a cost overrun of $846 million and a 3-year delay. GAO identified that the lack of systems engineering discipline early in a program is one of the contributors to significant quality problems later in the program development. In addition, manufacturing problems and higher product costs resulted from the lack of process controls and supplier quality problems. GAO also stated that the DoD quality management organizations provide minimal oversight of the prime contractor activities and do not collect the data in a way that would allow the study of trends to provide decision makers with information about systemic quality-related problems. GAO further stated that successful commercial companies used disciplined, well-defined, and institutionalized practices to improve quality. GAO recommended that "the Secretary of Defense takes actions to set achievable requirements for new weapon system development, oversee and expand initiatives that could improve quality, and use data to assess contractor performance and weapon system quality."

In 2010, GAO reported quality management as one of the nine basic risk areas for DoD manufacturing. GAO reviewed quality management practices for four weapons systems including the Joint Air-to-Surface Standoff Missile, Exoatmospheric Kill Vehicle, Electromagnetic Aircraft Launch System, and H-1 helicopter upgrade. GAO reported examples of poor quality assurance, which affected the manufacturing and reliability of the end products. The Joint Air-to-Surface Standoff Missile program office shifted the responsibility for ensuring quality and reliability of the program from the Government to the contractor. Specifically, the prime contractor was relying on the subtier suppliers to self-report and was not providing effective oversight, ultimately leading to defective parts. In the Exoatmospheric Kill Vehicle program, rework and late discovery of issues were directly linked to poor supplier QA. The prime contractor did not flow down the QA requirements for space programs to the subcontractor, which led to recurring quality issues. Additionally, there was insufficient training on the quality control standards that should have been required and institutionalized.

In June 2011, GAO issued a report, GAO-11-404, regarding the impact of part quality problems on missile defense programs. GAO reviewed several National Aeronautics and Space Administration (NASA) and DoD satellite and missile defense programs with mature designs and projected high costs to examine quality problems related to parts and manufacturing processes and materials. The programs that GAO reviewed include:

- Advanced Extremely High Frequency (AEHF) Satellites,
- Global Positioning System (GPS) Block IIF,
- Mobile User Objective System (MUOS),
- Space-Based Infrared System (SBIRS) High Program,
- Space-Based Space Surveillance (SBSS) Block 10,
- Aegis Ballistic Missile Defense (BMD),
- Ground-Based Midcourse Defense (GMD),
- Space Tracking and Surveillance System (STSS), and
- Targets and Countermeasures systems.

The report stated that part-quality problems were identified in all programs that were reviewed, some of which contributed to significant cost overruns, schedule delays, and reduced system reliability and availability. For instance, during system-level thermal vacuum testing of the Air Force's AEHF satellite program, defective electronic parts caused a power regulating unit to fail, resulting in a launch delay of almost 2 years and a cost of at least $250 million to retest.

In addition, the Missile Defense Agency's (MDA) GMD program encountered problems with an electronic part in the telemetry unit of the Exoatmospheric Kill Vehicle used to transmit flight test data during final assembly and test operations, resulting in the cancellation of a major flight test, a delay of 25 months, and a cost of $19 million. Another MDA program, STSS, also encountered problems with defective electronic parts during system-level testing and integration, resulting in a cost of about $7 million and contributing to a 17-month launch delay of two demonstration satellites and delayed participation in Ballistic Missile Defense System (BMDS) testing. GAO concluded that the Government's attention to and oversight of parts quality had declined for various reasons and there was no mechanism in place to periodically evaluate the condition of parts quality on major space and missile defense programs. GAO recommended that DoD and NASA implement a new process for such reporting and provide the results of these reports to Congress.

In November 2013, GAO issued a report, GAO-14-122, highlighting the Navy's practice of accepting ships with significant deficiencies. In 2009, the Navy initiated the Back-to-Basics initiative to establish a quality performance standard that set forth common quality requirements to be included in shipbuilding contracts with the intent of improving Navy oversight of ship construction. However, the Navy had not implemented consistent and adequate quality management requirements in its acquisition processes. As a result, unclear roles and responsibilities throughout the Naval Sea Systems (NAVSEA) organizations made it difficult to provide proper quality assurance oversight. GAO recommended, among other things, that the Secretary of the Navy provide guidance on contract quality requirements.

On September 30, 2013, DoD OIG issued a report, DODIG-2013-140, "Quality Assurance Assessment of the F-35 Lightning II Program," which identified a multitude of deficiencies related to inadequate quality assurance practices, insufficient quality requirement flow down, and lack of systems engineering rigor applied to the design and manufacturing processes for DoD's largest and most visible program.

Quality management system deficiencies identified by GAO and DoD OIG reports include the following:

- inconsistent process review at key decision points across programs,
- quality metrics not consolidated in a manner that helps decision makers identify and evaluate systemic quality problems,
- insufficient workforce knowledge,
- inadequate resources to provide sufficient oversight, and
- ineffective supplier oversight.

The milestone decision authorities and program managers are responsible for the overall success of the program, but in accordance with DoD Directive 5105.64, "Defense Contract Management Agency (DCMA)," January 10, 2013, Federal Acquisition Regulation (FAR) 42.302, "Contract Administration Functions," and 46.104, "Contract Administration Office Responsibilities," DCMA is the quality assurance oversight authority.

Evaluation Process

We evaluated the quality management practices used throughout the DoD acquisition community using a top-down evaluation approach. We also evaluated regulatory requirements to determine their applicability to DoD acquisition programs. Next, the team evaluated the policies and procedures related to quality management systems at the Office of the Secretary of Defense (OSD) and within DoD Components.

We evaluated OSD and DoD Component-level documents including DoD Instruction 5000.02, "Operation of the Defense Acquisition System," December 08, 2008; Interim DoD Instruction 5000.02, "Operation of the Defense Acquisition System," November 25, 2013; Defense Federal Acquisition Regulation Supplement (DFARS); DFARS Procedures, Guidance, and Information (PGIs); the Defense Acquisition Guidebook (DAG); and other DoD Component-specific documents. We interviewed personnel representing each Military Department and various DoD organizations to understand quality assurance practices across DoD. Specifically, we interviewed representatives of the following DoD Components:

- Army,
- Navy,
- Air Force,

- Office of the Under Secretary of Defense for Acquisition, Technology and Logistics (OUSD[AT&L]),

- MDA, and

- DCMA.

Based on these interviews, we evaluated the QA policies and procedures against industry best practices. For each organization, we evaluated the acquisition-related policies, procedures, and guidance to determine if they were sufficient to ensure that quality management activities were implemented throughout the acquisition life cycle of the programs. See Appendix A for additional scope and methodology.

Evaluation Criteria

Quality management practices throughout the Department of Defense were evaluated using Government and private industry quality management standards as our evaluation criteria and as a reference. The International Organization for Standardization (ISO) 9000 series was the primary source of evaluation criteria used; however, also referenced were a Navy study of quality management best practices, the Navy Total Quality Leadership Office (TQLO) Publication No. 92-02, "Three Experts on Quality Management: Philip B. Crosby, W. Edwards Deming, Joseph M. Juran," July 1992, the Aerospace Standard (AS) 9100, and an industrially recognized quality management handbook, "Juran's Quality Handbook" (5th Edition). A common theme found in each quality management resource cited is the importance placed on leadership involvement and feedback mechanisms to facilitate the continual improvement of quality management systems.

Our primary source, the internationally recognized ISO 9000 series of standards, originally published in 1987, went through a major revision in 2000. The most recently revised standards identify the requirements, definitions, and processes necessary to establish an effective and efficient quality management system. For instance, ISO 9000:2005 identifies basic concepts and definitions for quality management systems, ISO 9001:2008 identifies requirements for quality management systems, and ISO 9004:2009 provides guidance for continual improvement of quality management systems. The ISO 9000 series of standards is based on the following eight quality management principles:

1. Customer Focus
2. Leadership
3. Involvement of people
4. Process approach

5. System approach to management

6. Continual improvement

7. Factual approach to decision-making

8. Mutually beneficial supplier relationships

These principles highlight the importance of leadership involvement, the establishment of common goals, and organizational direction with respect to quality management. They also emphasize the need for feedback mechanisms to facilitate continual process improvement and support a fact-based approach to decision making.

Our secondary source, The AS9100, "Quality Management Systems – Requirements for Aviation, Space, and Defense Organizations," is based on ISO 9001 requirements supplemented with additional quality system requirements established by the aerospace industry.

Additional sources used as part of our evaluation criteria were the Navy Total Quality Leadership Office (TQLO) Publication No. 92-02, "Three Experts on Quality Management: Philip B. Crosby, W. Edwards Deming, Joseph M. Juran," July 1992, and Juran's Quality Handbook (5th Edition). The Navy TQLO publication summarizes the best practices developed by world renowned quality management experts who have set quality management best practices for more than 50 years ; Philip B. Crosby, W. Edwards Deming, and Joseph M. Juran. Emphasized within the publication are the importance of top level leadership involvement and effective feedback mechanisms for continual improvement of quality management system. It also emphasizes the fact that in order to facilitate the successful implementation of a standards-based quality management system, a cultural shift is often required within organizations, and must start with top level leadership, and be embraced by all participants. Furthermore, the publication highlights performance measurement as being important to quality improvement efforts. Performance measurement data must be communicated through feedback mechanisms to leadership in order to facilitate improvement in quality management. Juran's Quality authored by Joseph M. Juran, provided us additional details describing the need for continual process improvement and identifies feedback mechanisms as a critical contributor to quality management success.

This collection of quality management best practices provided us with the criteria required to evaluate quality management practices across the DoD.

Finding A

DoD Lacks Overarching Quality Management Policy and Guidance

Although numerous policies related to quality assurance exist and are dispersed throughout the DoD, the OUSD(AT&L) has not established overarching policy and guidance specifically related to quality management responsibilities and procedures. As a result, quality management practices have not been consistently implemented across DoD Components to ensure effective and efficient quality assurance oversight of DoD acquisition programs.

Discussion

Quality assurance, as defined by International Organization for Standardization (ISO) 9000, "International Standard: Quality Management Systems – Fundamentals and Vocabulary," is a component of quality management that is "focused on providing confidence that quality requirements will be fulfilled." Quality assurance processes are focused on the inspection of final products and the processes that contribute to their production. Quality management, on the other hand, is defined as an overall set of "coordinated activities to direct and control an organization with regard to quality." ISO 9000 states that quality assurance is a subset of an overall quality management methodology, which also includes the establishment of quality policy, quality objectives, quality planning, quality control, and quality improvement.

In accordance with DoD Directive 5134.01, "Under Secretary of Defense for Acquisition, Technology and Logistics (USD[AT&L])," OUSD(AT&L) is responsible for establishing acquisition policies for all DoD Components. DoD has issued a number of policies that contain quality assurance-related provisions pertaining to acquisition programs including DoD Directive 5000.01, "Defense Acquisition System," DoD Instruction 5000.02, "Operation of the Defense Acquisition System," DoD Instruction 5000.35, "Defense Acquisition Regulations (DAR) System," DoD Directive 5105.64, and the DAG.

DoD Directive 5000.01 is the foundational policy document that provides management principles and mandatory policies and procedures for the execution of all acquisition programs. DoD Directive 5000.01 also authorizes the publication of DoD Instruction 5000.02, which briefly addresses quality assurance as it relates to risk management. Enclosure 3, "System Engineering," of Interim DoD Instruction 5000.02 contains a brief description relating to overall quality management of DoD acquisition programs. It states that it is the program manager's responsibility to ensure that manufacturing and producibility risks are controlled and acceptable throughout the life cycle of an acquisition program. DoD Instruction 5000.35 establishes policy and assigns responsibilities for the management and operation of the DAR system. DoD Directive 5105.64 establishes DCMA's mission, organization and management, responsibilities and functions, relationships, authorities, and administration in accordance with applicable statutory and regulatory requirements. DAG clause 11.3.3, "Quality Management," and the Defense Acquisition University website define Quality Management System (QMS)-related terms; however, these sources only supply guidance, and their use is not mandated. Therefore, the OUSD(AT&L), Military Departments, MDA, and DCMA each have their own interpretation of how to implement a QMS.

Although there is no overarching QM policy at the OUSD(AT&L) level, quality assurance policies and authority are dispersed throughout DoD. Policies related to QA activities such as DFARS and PGI which are overseen by the Defense Procurement and Acquisition Policy (DPAP); contract administration QA policies which are overseen by DCMA; and manufacturing and production policies which are overseen by the Deputy Assistant Secretary of Defense for Systems Engineering (DASD[SE]).

Additionally, OUSD(AT&L) is not actively involved in quality management oversight of acquisition programs. OUSD(AT&L) monitors Major Defense Acquisition Programs (MDAPs) through the Defense Acquisition Executive Summary (DAES) process. However, the DAES process does not require a proactive evaluation of QA metrics to ensure program quality issues are identified and resolved prior to the realization of a negative cost, schedule, or performance impact. Furthermore, OUSD(AT&L) does not have a dedicated organization responsible for quality management system policies to ensure that quality requirements are consistently applied to contracts and that quality management methods are effectively implemented across acquisition programs. Top-level leadership involvement and commitment are necessary to ensure effective and efficient application of quality management practices through policies and guidance across DoD.

Variations in quality management practices throughout the Military Departments can be exemplified by the following cases. The Army has top-level QMS policy, Army Regulation 702-11, "Army Quality Program," which requires each Army commands, units, service component commands, and acquisition programs to establish its own quality requirements. Similarly, the Air Force established top-level QMS policy Air Force Instruction 63-501, "Air Force Acquisition Quality Program," and also delegated the quality related matters to a lower level within the component, the program executive officers. Although the Secretary of the Navy (SECNAV) Instruction 5000.2E, "Department of the Navy Implementation and Operation of the Defense Acquisition System and the Joint Capability," briefly described the requirement for quality assurance and referenced ISO 9001, "Quality Management Systems - Requirements," it is unclear who (the program manager or the contractors) is ultimately responsible for establishing QMS. Each Navy component; such as NAVSEA, Naval Air Systems Command (NAVAIR), Naval Supply Systems Command (NAVSUP), Space and Naval Warfare Systems Command (SPAWAR), and Marine Corps (MARCORPS); has implemented QMS differently.

As highlighted in multiple GAO and DoD IG reports, quality management system-related problems have resulted in major cost overruns, schedule delays, and reduced system performance. Top-level management commitment to product quality is necessary to ensure that the DoD acquisition community considers quality management as a major contributor to a successful program and takes action accordingly. The Navy's TQLO Publication No. 92-02 highlighted the importance of top-level management commitment to quality as well as the need for common language for clarity and consistency of quality management policies across the organization to achieve improvement.

Conclusion

Despite the abundance of policies and guidance related to quality assurance throughout DoD, policy and guidance specifically related quality management is inadequate. Additionally, lack of leadership emphasis and attention to overall quality management in acquisition programs often results in quality issues not being handled until late in the acquisition process when the cost to correct such problems is greatly increased.

Recommendation A – Management Comments and Our Response

We recommend that the Office of the Under Secretary of Defense for Acquisition, Technology and Logistics:

Recommendation 1

Establish within AT&L a dedicated quality management function to provide leadership and oversight of quality management system requirements across DoD acquisition programs.

AT&L Comments

AT&L did not concur and stated:

> While we agree there are benefits to central leadership, it already exists. As discussed above, the DASD for Systems Engineering already provides the overarching quality management function for defense acquisition. These functions include specific areas such as reliability, mission assurance, and overall systems engineering. DASD(SE) also provides functional leadership to more than 40,000 defense acquisition professionals in the DoD Engineering (ENG) and Production, Quality, and Manufacturing (PQM) workforce. DASD(SE) also serves as the Defense Standardization Executive. Supporting administrative, contracting, and technical aspects of QA/QM across the enterprise are appropriately led by the AT&L elements described above.

Our Response

We acknowledge the fact that QA/QM falls within the purview of DASD(SE); however, it is scattered throughout the enterprise and being led by different functional elements instead of as a dedicated quality management function. DODI 5134.16, "Deputy Assistant Secretary of Defense for Systems Engineering (DASD[SE])," does not clearly give DASD(SE) the authority to establish quality management policies and provide oversight. As identified in our report, there is no overarching QM policy at the OUSD(AT&L) level that ensures major defense acquisition program quality management systems are evaluated by AT&L leadership throughout the program lifecycle. Despite current policies and guidance related to quality assurance throughout DoD; they have been insufficient based on evidence of major cost overruns, schedule delays, and reduced system performance which were attributed to quality management system-related issues. Additionally, the lack of leadership emphasis and attention to overall quality management in acquisition programs from the inception of the program through deployment often results in quality issues not being addressed until late in the acquisition process. We request additional comments from AT&L on this recommendation.

Recommendation 2

Provide clear and concise quality management system definitions and policies for all DoD major acquisition programs that emphasize the importance of a robust quality management program throughout the entire acquisition life cycle.

AT&L Comments

AT&L did not concur and stated:

> While we agree that clear and concise definitions and policies are important, again we already have sufficient, extensive policy and regulatory structures in place according to each aspect of quality management, including quality standards, reliability oversight, systems engineering, and testing. For example, to align with industry and maintain current best practices, the DoD leverages industry standards for definitions and processes, which are commonly known as ISO 9000. Defense Acquisition Guidebook, Chapter 11, Program Management Activities, Section 11.3.3 Quality Management provides clear reference to those standards definitions and provides additional best practices applicable to DoD acquisition.

Our Response

We strongly believe that dedicated leadership at AT&L is required to establish clear and concise DoD level quality management policies to promote improved program supply chain performance throughout the DoD acquisition lifecycle. The Defense Acquisition Guidebook (DAG) provides only guidance and its use is not mandated. Under OUSD(AT&L), the Office of the Deputy Assistant Secretary of Defense for Systems Engineering is responsible for identifying, systems engineering gaps and deficiencies early in the acquisition process, establishing policy and guidance to close those gaps, and promoting cost effective and successful weapon systems development. However, OUSD (AT&L) does not have a similar dedicated organization focusing on quality assurance. Currently, quality assurance policies and authority are scattered throughout DoD. Policies exist that are related to QA activities such as DFARS and PGI which are overseen by the Defense Procurement and Acquisition Policy (DPAP); contract administration QA policies which are overseen by DCMA; and manufacturing and production policies which are overseen by the Deputy Assistant Secretary of Defense for Systems Engineering (DASD[SE]). In several instances, program offices did not establish communication channels with DCMA to effectively provide Government oversight but instead deferred their quality oversight responsibilities to DCMA. In addition, DCMA is usually involved at the tail end of the acquisition lifecycle, while the quality management processes should have been implemented during the earlier part of the acquisition lifecycle. We request additional comments from AT&L on this recommendation.

Finding B

Ineffective Feedback Mechanisms to Improve the Quality Management System

DoD and its Components did not have effective feedback mechanisms in place to influence positive change in quality management policies and processes. Our evaluation did not find evidence that information needed to detect trends, identify threats and opportunities, and evaluate performance is being reported to those responsible for issuing quality management policies throughout DoD.

Discussion

The OUSD(AT&L) does not have an oversight office responsible for DoD quality management systems to evaluate program supply chain performance trends and to evaluate and revise policies, procedures, and guidance. Responsibility and accountability are necessary at the top level to evaluate quality trends across acquisition programs based on performance feedback. The results of the evaluation should be used by leadership to update or issue policies and guidance for continual improvement of QMS.

Not only are ineffective feedback mechanisms evident at the OUSD(AT&L) level, but they were also an issue at other DoD Components. For instance, the Army officials identified that data needed for effective feedback, such as product quality deficiency data across DoD, are not consolidated in a manner that can be used to identify problems, trends, and recurring deficiencies and to fully evaluate systemic enterprise-level quality performance. Additionally, the Air Force has no effective feedback mechanism at the headquarters level to evaluate the effectiveness of quality management policies and subsequently make necessary adjustments to the policies.

In accordance with SECNAV Instruction 4855.3C, "Product Data Reporting and Evaluation Program," the Navy, specifically NAVSEA, establishes and maintains an automated information system called Product Data Reporting and Evaluation Program (PDREP) to record and maintain the supplier performance information. This system is also used by the other DoD Components such as DCMA, DLA, and

Army. However, other military commands, such as the Air Force and NAVAIR, use an automated system, Joint Deficiency Reporting System (JDRS), to report supplier performance data to PDREP. The PDREP automated information system is designed only to provide supplier performance data to manage and monitor the performance of the supply chain. Currently, there is no policy stating that OSD or DoD Components are required to use data from the PDREP to establish or revise QMS policies.

In addition to the problems within the Military Departments, ineffective feedback mechanism were also evident between program management offices (PMOs) and organizations performing quality assurance-related Contract Administration Services (CAS). DoD Directive 5105.64 requires DCMA to perform CAS functions in accordance with FAR Part 42, "Contract Administration and Audit Services," and DFARS Part 242, "Contract Administration and Audit Services." DCMA is required to obtain information necessary to prepare risk-based surveillance and program support plans in accordance with FAR, DFARS, and DCMA instructions. Although PMOs are ultimately responsible for the success of their programs, these regulations and instructions do not require DCMA to solicit concurrence from the PMOs to proceed with its final quality assurance oversight approach. A more collaborative effort between DCMA and PMOs is necessary to ensure that program risks are properly addressed in their quality assurance oversight plans. Proper identification of program risk is necessary to ensure that resources are allocated appropriately in order to mitigate the risk of discovering quality issues at a later phase of system development.

Conclusion

The need for effective feedback mechanisms to institute continual process improvement has been identified in the industry as one of the critical contributors to quality management success. Quality management requires extensive decision making, covering a wide range of subject matter at all levels within the hierarchy of an organization. Information is needed to detect major trends, identify threats and opportunities, and evaluate performance. Action must be taken based on this information in order to further improve quality, but this cannot be done unless proper feedback mechanisms are established.

Recommendation B – Management Comments and Our Response

We recommend that the Office of the Under Secretary of Defense for Acquisition, Technology and Logistics:

Recommendation 1

Establish quality assurance verification processes throughout the acquisition life cycle that promote effective program and supply chain quality management systems.

AT&L Comments

AT&L partially concurred and stated:

> DoD already has explicit processes to verify that the items we acquire meet the contractual requirements and standards we establish. QA verification is part of DCMA's contract administration responsibilities. DCMA has over 30 QA specific policies at http://www.dcma.mil/policy/ covering planning, contract review, surveillance, QA system audits, product acceptance, and overhaul/ maintenance as well as other polices on manufacturing and production, production surveillance, and risk management.

> Additionally, Better Buying Power 2.0 initiative on instituting a superior supplier incentive program specifically includes quality as a factor. The Navy has rolled out its pilot program in June 2014. Building the results of the pilot, OUSD(AT&L) hopes to improve and expand the program to the other components.

> These processes are working poorly in many cases right now for a very simple reason: a shortage of trained and qualified acquisition professionals in the quality field. This has several consequences: program offices lack effective quality advocacy in routine decision-making and important dimensions of quality process implementation - most notably right now in value chain quality processes - are very difficult to achieve.

Our Response

AT&L's response focuses on the inspection and surveillance processes used during product manufacturing. The intent of the recommendation was for AT&L to establish DoD level quality management policies that define quality performance data deliverables throughout in the acquisition process, which could prevent unnecessary program costs. This is similar to data needed by Milestone Decision Authority (MDA) to make program milestone decisions during the acquisition process. We request additional comments from AT&L on this recommendation.

Recommendation 2

Establish standardized reporting requirements for quality assurance metrics throughout DoD to obtain the information needed to detect trends, identify threats and opportunities, and evaluate program performance.

AT&L Comments

AT&L partially concurred and stated:

> DCMA's SRS etool already tracks over 25,000 facilities performance and is used by over 300 PEOs and Buying Commands to identify good performing contractors and for us to develop optimum risk-based surveillance plans at the lowest costs to the DoD.

> Also, as described above, DoD acquisition contracts for a large array of products and services with greatly varying aspects of what constitutes quality or how to measure it. Even with respect to weapon systems and MDAPs at the top level, there are effectiveness and suitability OT &E ratings as well as standardized Key Performance Parameters to evaluate the whole portfolio. However, detailed quality metrics for satellites are very different than those for armored ground vehicles or ships. At that level, programs should continue to use industry standards that are applicable to the product in question. The DAES review process is flexible for this very reason to allow all parties to raise concerns appropriate to the type of system in question rather than standardizing on more specific metrics. The Components and OSD continue to examine and improve how we can better measure performance, including the kind of quality issues that have arisen in the past.

> That said, I would not argue that we make the most use of the data we have or the managerial discipline to assure it is accurate because of the human capital problem cited above. We have a long way to go to make data-driven quality considerations a routine part of programmatic processes and the place to start is to assure that we have the staff expertise in place to use the data.

Our Response

We strongly believe that high level quality assurance performance metrics should be standardized and reported for major acquisition programs. As a result of our evaluation, we understand the tools that DCMA has in place to determine supplier performance. We are also aware of the fact that specific product quality requirements may differ vastly between different types of weapon systems. However, there are some common quality assurance metrics that are primary indicators of supplier performance, such as the number of non-conformances, engineering changes, corrective actions, and waivers and deviations per month.

Such quality performance data should be compiled and provided to AT&L to promote proactive quality management practices. We request AT&L to provide additional comments on this recommendation.

Recommendation 3

Establish policy that ensures DCMA policies and risk-based quality assurance oversight decisions are reviewed, understood, and agreed to by the PMOs.

AT&L Comments

AT&L partially concurred and stated:

> For programs, "GCQA is conducted by the program manager and Defense Contract Management Agency (DCMA) as identified in contract administration delegations to DCMA by the Contracting Officer" (see DAG 11.3.3). Here the problem is not in our policies per se but in implementation decisions. We need to continue working towards having a sufficient workforce with the time, training, and incentives to better communicate with DCMA to assess and prioritize the costs and benefits of different levels of quality and contractor oversight. This includes the size and training of the oversight workforce in the Components and OSD as well as execution discussions in the PMOs. The Department has worked hard to rebuild the acquisition workforce after years of outsourcing and neglect from past acquisition "reforms" with some success, but more is needed. Sequestration and other budgetary pressures have been the major impediment to improvement on this front, and AT &L continues to improve this situation as resources allow.

Our Response

We believe that AT&L needs to establish policies that ensure PMOs are appropriately delegating the level of DCMA surveillance required. Currently, DCMA's instructions do not require DCMA to solicit concurrence from the PMOs in determining the level of quality assurance oversight. PMOs are ultimately responsible for the success of their programs and should define the level of product quality assurance oversight required by DCMA based on program risk and weapon system criticality. We request AT&L to provide additional comments on this recommendation.

Appendix A

Scope and Methodology

We conducted this evaluation from April 22, 2013, through June 2014, in accordance with the Council of the Inspectors General on Integrity and Efficiency, "Quality Standards for Inspection and Evaluation." Those standards require that we plan and perform the evaluation to obtain sufficient, appropriate evidence to provide a reasonable basis for our findings and conclusions based on our evaluation objectives. We believe that the evidence obtained provides a reasonable basis for our findings and conclusions based on our evaluation objectives.

The objective of this evaluation was to evaluate overarching quality management policies and processes of DoD and Government-performed quality assurance oversight of defense acquisition programs. This evaluation was self-initiated due to gaps and deficiencies in overarching policy related to quality management, practices, and oversight as identified by several GAO and DoD OIG reports. To evaluate the quality management practices across the DoD, we evaluated top-level policies and procedures across DoD Components. We evaluated the quality management practices across the DoD by starting at OSD-level quality management related policies including DoDI 500.02, DFARS/PGI, and DAG. In addition, we interviewed officials from the Army, the Navy, the Air Force, OUSD(AT&L), MDA, and DCMA and evaluated their policies relevant to quality management processes.

Use of Computer-Processed Data

We did not use computer-processed data to perform this evaluation.

Appendix B

Prior Coverage

Most recently, the Government Accountability Office (GAO) and the Department of Defense Inspector General (DoD IG) issued 10 reports discussing quality assurance deficiencies within DoD acquisition programs. Unrestricted GAO reports can be accessed over the Internet at http://www.gao.gov. Unrestricted DoD IG reports can be accessed at http://www.dodig.mil/pubs/index.cfm.

GAO

Report No. GAO-14-122, "Navy Ship Building: Opportunities Exist to Improve Practices Affecting Quality," November 19, 2013

Report No. GAO-12-83, "Defense Contract Management Agency: Amid Ongoing Efforts to Rebuild Capacity, Several Factors Present Challenges in Meeting its Missions," November 3, 2011

Report No. GAO-11-404, "Periodic Assessment Needed to Correct Parts Quality Problems in Major Programs," June 24, 2011

Report No. GAO-11-61R, "Additional Guidance Needed to Improve Visibility into the Structure and Management of Major Weapon System Subcontracts," October 28, 2010

Report No. GAO-10-439, "DoD Can Achieve Better Outcomes by Standardizing the Way Manufacturing Risks Are Managed," April 22, 2010

Report No. GAO-08-294, "Best Practices: Increased Focus on Requirements and Oversight Needed to Improve DoD's Acquisition Environment and Weapon System Quality," February 1, 2008

DoD IG

Report No. DODIG-2013-140, "Quality Assurance Assessment of the F-35 Lightning II Program," September 30, 2013

Report No. D-2013-069, "Defense Contract Management Agency Santa Ana Quality Assurance Oversight Needs Improvement," April 19, 2013

Report No. D-2011-088, "Ballistic Testing for Interceptor Body Armor Inserts Needs Improvement," August 1, 2011

Report No. D-2011-030, "Ballistic Testing and Product Quality Surveillance for the Interceptor Body Armor - Vest Components Need Improvement," January 3, 2011

Management Comments

Office of the Under Secretary of Defense for Acquisition, Technology and Logistics

OFFICE OF THE ASSISTANT SECRETARY OF DEFENSE
3015 DEFENSE PENTAGON
WASHINGTON, DC 20301-3015

OCT 17 2014

ACQUISITION

MEMORANDUM FOR DOD INSPECTOR GENERAL

THROUGH: DIRECTOR, ACQUISITION RESOURCES AND ANALYSIS

SUBJECT: Comments on DoD IG's Evaluation of Government Quality Assurance Oversight for DoD Acquisition Programs (Project No. D2013-DTOTAD-0001)

Thank you for the opportunity to review and comment on your draft report, Evaluation of Government Quality Assurance Oversight for DoD Acquisition Programs (Project No. D2013-DTOTAD-0001). Attached are itemized comments to the recommendations in the draft.

Generally, I agree with the principles outlined in the report, but to a large extent the Department already has clearly established leadership, policies, and processes in place to provide those fundamentals. Implementation of policies and processes is another matter, and it is here that I believe the root of our quality issues lie.

The challenge your report misses is ensuring we have a sufficiently sized, qualified, and trained acquisition workforce to follow the fundamentals already in place. The Department has worked hard to rebuild the acquisition workforce with some success after years of outsourcing and neglect from past acquisition "reform" but more progress is needed. Sequestration and other budgetary pressures have been the major impediment to improvement on many fronts, to include quality assurance and quality management.

Katrina McFarland

Attachment:
1. ASD(A) Comments on Draft Report for Project No. D2013-DTOTAD-0001

cc:
USD(AT&L)
PDUSD(AT&L)
D(DCMA)
DASD(Systems Engineering)
D(DPAP)
███████████ (DCMA), Chair, DFARS Quality Assurance Committee

Office of the Under Secretary of Defense for Acquisition, Technology and Logistics (cont'd)

ASD(A) Comments on Draft Report for Project No. D2013-DTOTAD-0001

Summary

AT&L generally agrees with the principles outline in the report, but to a large extent the Department already has clearly established leadership, policies, and processes in place to provide those fundamentals. The challenge missing in the report is ensuring we have a sufficient, qualified, and trained acquisition workforce to follow the fundamentals already in place. The Department has worked hard to rebuild the acquisition workforce with some success after years of outsourcing and neglect from past acquisition "reforms" but more progress is needed. Sequestration and other budgetary pressures have been the major impediment to improvement on many fronts, to include quality assurance and quality management.

Background

OUSD(AT&L) is responsible for delivering quality to the warfighter across all DoD acquisition. Quality management and quality assurance requires ongoing oversight and continuous improvement processes which must always be balanced with cost. While quality deficiencies can have significant costs as highlighted by your assessment and other GAO and DoD IG reports, excessive quality assurance also drives up contracting costs. In today's fiscal environment and always, the acquisition workforce needs to weigh both costs equally.

Quality management and quality assurance best practices vary greatly depending on what is acquired—including differences among different supplies, equipment, and services—and the DoD's acquisitions are spread widely across these different types. In fiscal year 2013, DoD contracted obligations totaled $318.7 billion (FY15$). Supplies and Equipment were $152.6 billion, or 48%, and contracted Services were $166.1 billion, or 52%. Within Supplies and Equipment, weapons systems (e.g., Aircraft, Ship/Submarines, Land Vehicles) was the largest portfolio, but still only one-third of the obligations at $55 billion. Within Services, Research and Development was the second largest portfolio after Knowledge-Based Services at $30 billion. See Performance of the Defense Acquisition System, 2014, p. 5 for complete spend breakdown. http://www.acq.osd.mil/docs/Performance-of-Defense-Acquisition-System-2014.pdf.

Quality management (QM) and quality assurance (QA) requires the involvement of specialties across the acquisition workforce. While my office is responsible for overseeing all defense acquisitions, specific overarching responsibility in the Department for quality and management of production and manufacturing risks fall under system engineering and thus the purview of the OUSD(AT&L)/ASD(Research & Engineering)/System Engineering office. The Defense Contract Management Agency (DCMA) is responsible for contract administration across the enterprise, which includes QA processes and execution. What DCMA administers depends on what is in the contract, and contracting practices, including those for QA, are guided by the Federal Acquisition Regulations (FAR) and the Defense FAR Supplement (DFARS), which is overseen by the Defense Acquisition Regulations System under the OUSD(AT&L)/Defense Procurement and Acquisition Policy (DPAP) office. Lastly, QM is the responsibility of program management by the acquiring Component.

DoD IG Recommendation A.1
Establish within OUSD(AT&L) a dedicated quality management function to provide leadership and oversight of quality management system requirements across DoD acquisition programs.

Office of the Under Secretary of Defense for Acquisition, Technology and Logistics (cont'd)

ASD(A) Comments on Draft Report for Project No. D2013-DTOTAD-0001

Already exists: While we agree there are benefits to central leadership, it already exists. As discussed above, the DASD for Systems Engineering already provides the overarching quality management function for defense acquisition. These functions include specific areas such as reliability, mission assurance, and overall systems engineering. DASD(SE) also provides functional leadership to more than 40,000 defense acquisition professionals in the DoD Engineering (ENG) and Production, Quality, and Manufacturing (PQM) workforce. DASD(SE) also serves as the Defense Standardization Executive. Supporting administrative, contracting, and technical aspects of QA/QM across the enterprise are appropriately led by the AT&L elements described above.

DoD IG Recommendation A.2
Provide clear and concise quality management system definitions and policies for all DoD major acquisition programs that emphasize the importance of a robust quality management program throughout the entire acquisition life cycle.

Already exists: While we agree that clear and concise definitions and policies are important, again we already have sufficient, extensive policy and regulatory structures in place according to each aspect of quality management, including quality standards, reliability oversight, systems engineering, and testing. For example, to align with industry and maintain current best practices, the DoD leverages industry standards for definitions and processes, which are commonly known as ISO 9000. Defense Acquisition Guidebook, Chapter 11, Program Management Activities, Section 11.3.3 Quality Management provides clear reference to those standards definitions and provides additional best practices applicable to DoD acquisition.

DoD IG Recommendation B.1
Establish quality assurance verification processes throughout the acquisition life cycle that promote effective program and supply chain quality management systems.

Partially Concur: DoD already has explicit processes to verify that the items we acquire meet the contractual requirements and standards we establish. QA verification is part of DCMA's contract administration responsibilities. DCMA has over 30 QA specific policies at http://www.dcma.mil/policy/ covering planning, contract review, surveillance, QA system audits, product acceptance, and overhaul/maintenance as well as other polices on manufacturing and production, production surveillance, and risk management.

Additionally, Better Buying Power 2.0 initiative on instituting a superior supplier incentive program specifically includes quality as a factor. The Navy has rolled out its pilot program in

June 2014. Building the results of the pilot, OUSD(AT&L) hopes to improve and expand the program to the other components.

These processes are working poorly in many cases right now for a very simple reason: a shortage of trained and qualified acquisition professionals in the quality field. This has several consequences: program offices lack effective quality advocacy in routine decision-making and important dimensions of quality process implementation — most notably right now in value-chain quality processes — are very difficult to achieve.

Office of the Under Secretary of Defense for Acquisition, Technology and Logistics (cont'd)

ASD(A) Comments on Draft Report for Project No. D2013-DTOTAD-0001

DoD IG Recommendation B.2
Establish standardized reporting requirements for quality metrics throughout DoD to obtain the information needed to detect trends, identify threats and opportunities, and evaluate program performance.

Partially Concur: DCMA's SRS etool already tracks over 25,000 facilities performance and is used by over 300 PEOs and Buying Commands to identify good performing contractors and for us to develop optimum risk-based surveillance plans at the lowest costs to the DoD.

Also, as described above, DoD acquisition contracts for a large array of products and services with greatly varying aspects of what constitutes quality or how to measure it. Even with respect to weapon systems and MDAPs at the top level, there are effectiveness and suitability OT&E ratings as well as standardized Key Performance Parameters to evaluate the whole portfolio. However, detailed quality metrics for satellites are very different than those for armored ground vehicles or ships. At that level, programs should continue to use industry standards that are applicable to the product in question. The DAES review process is flexible for this very reason—to allow all parties to raise concerns appropriate to the type of system in question rather than standardizing on more specific metrics. The Components and OSD continue to examine and improve how we can better measure performance, including the kind of quality issues that have arisen in the past.

That said, I would not argue that we make the most use of the data we have or the managerial discipline to assure it is accurate because of the human capital problem cited above. We have a long way to go to make data-driven quality considerations a routine part of programmatic processes and the place to start is to assure that we have the staff expertise in place to use the data.

DoD IG Recommendation B.3
Ensure Defense Contract Management Agency (DCMA) policies and risk-based quality assurance oversight decisions are reviewed, understood, and agreed to by both DCMA and program management offices (PMOs) to ensure resources are applied appropriately.

Partially Concur: For programs, "GCQA is conducted by the program manager and Defense Contract Management Agency (DCMA) as identified in contract administration delegations to

DCMA by the Contracting Officer" (see DAG 11.3.3). Here the problem is not in our policies per se but in implementation decisions. We need to continue working towards having a sufficient workforce with the time, training, and incentives to better communicate with DCMA to assess and prioritize the costs and benefits of different levels of quality and contractor oversight. This includes the size and training of the oversight workforce in the Components and OSD as well as execution discussions in the PMOs. The Department has worked hard to rebuild the acquisition workforce after years of outsourcing and neglect from past acquisition "reforms" with some success, but more is needed. Sequestration and other budgetary pressures have been the major impediment to improvement on this front, and AT&L continues to improve this situation as resources allow.

Acronyms and Abbreviations

AEHF	Advanced Extremely High Frequency
ASD(R&E)	Assistant Secretary of Defense for Research and Engineering
BMD	Ballistic Missile Defense
BMDS	Ballistic Missile Defense System
CAS	Contract Administration Services
DAES	Defense Acquisition Executive Summary
DAG	Procedures, Guidance, and Information
DAR	Defense Acquisition Regulation
DCMA	Defense Contract Management Agency
DFARS	Defense Federal Acquisition Regulation Supplement
DPAP	Defense Procurement and Acquisition Policy
FAR	Federal Acquisition Regulation
GAO	Government Accountability Office
GMD	Ground-Based Midcourse Defense
GPS	Global Positioning System
ISO	International Organization for Standardization
JDRS	Joint Deficiency Reporting System
MARCORPS	Marine Corps
MDA	Missile Defense Agency
MDAP	Major Defense Acquisition Program
MUOS	Mobile User Objective System
NASA	National Aeronautics and Space Administration
NAVAIR	Naval Air Systems Command
NAVSEA	Naval Sea Systems Command
NAVSUP	Naval Supply Systems Command
OIG	Office of Inspector General
OSD	Office of the Secretary of Defense
OUSD(AT&L)	Office of the Under Secretary of Defense for Acquisition, Technology and Logistics
PDREP	Product Data Reporting and Evaluation Program
PGI	Procedures, Guidance, and Information
PMO	Program Management Office
QA	Quality Assurance

Acronyms and Abbreviations (cont'd)

QM	Quality Management
QMS	Quality Management System
SBIRS	Space-Based Infrared System
SBSS	Space-Based Space Surveillance
SECNAV	Secretary of the Navy
SPAWAR	Space and Naval Warfare Systems Command
STSS	Space Tracking and Surveillance System
TQLO	Total Quality Leadership Office

Whistleblower Protection
U.S. Department of Defense

The Whistleblower Protection Enhancement Act of 2012 requires the Inspector General to designate a Whistleblower Protection Ombudsman to educate agency employees about prohibitions on retaliation, and rights and remedies against retaliation for protected disclosures. The designated ombudsman is the DoD Hotline Director. For more information on your rights and remedies against retaliation, visit www.dodig.mil/programs/whistleblower.

For more information about DoD IG reports or activities, please contact us:

Congressional Liaison
congressional@dodig.mil; 703.604.8324

Media Contact
public.affairs@dodig.mil; 703.604.8324

Monthly Update
dodigconnect-request@listserve.com

Reports Mailing List
dodig_report@listserve.com

Twitter
twitter.com/DoD_IG

DoD Hotline
dodig.mil/hotline